ZODIAC SIGNS

LIBRA

September 23 – October 23

Lydia Lukidis

AV2
www.av2books.com

AV2

Step 1
Go to **www.av2books.com**

Step 2
Enter this unique code
BAMWO5BU0

Step 3
Explore your interactive eBook!

AV2 is optimized for use on any device

Your interactive eBook comes with...

Contents
Browse a live contents page to easily navigate through resources

Audio
Listen to sections of the book read aloud

Videos
Watch informative video clips

Weblinks
Gain additional information for research

Try This!
Complete activities and hands-on experiments

Key Words
Study vocabulary, and complete a matching word activity

Quizzes
Test your knowledge

Slideshows
View images and captions

... and much, much more!

LIBRA

September 23 – October 23

Contents

Are You a Libra?

Do people find you charming? Are peace and justice important to you? If so, you might be a Libra. A Libra is someone who was born between September 23 and October 23.

Libra is a sign in the zodiac. This is a series of 12 **constellations** that run across the night sky. For centuries, people have used these groups of stars to tell the future. The study of the stars in this manner is called astrology.

Zodiac Chart

A person's zodiac sign is determined by his or her date of birth. Which sign matches your birthday?

It's in the Stars

The zodiac constellations form a circle around Earth. In one year, Earth makes a full **orbit** around the Sun. As it does this, the Sun appears to be in different places at set times. The zodiac constellations are found along the path the Sun follows.

Long ago, people used the Sun to tell the time of year. In late September, the Sun passed through the Libra constellation. People born then were said to be born under the sign of Libra.

Over time, the position of the constellations shifted. Even though the Sun now passes through Libra at a different time, the dates associated with the sign of Libra remain the same.

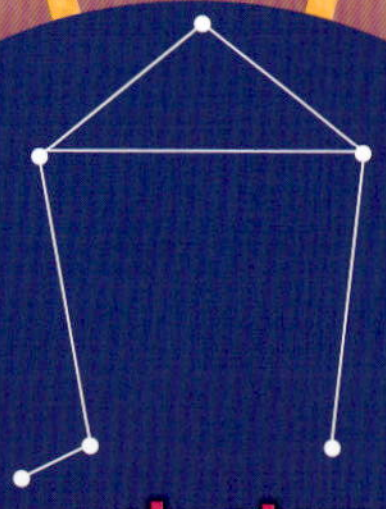

There are **six stars** in the main **Libra constellation**. At least **83 other stars** are found inside it.

Beta Librae is the **brightest** star in the Libra constellation. It is **five times bigger** than the Sun, and **twice** as **hot.**

Libra's main stars are said to resemble a weighing scale. This makes it the only zodiac constellation to represent an object.

The Myth of Libra

The ancient Greeks had stories about how each zodiac constellation came to be in the sky. Libra is linked to Astraea, a goddess of justice and purity.

The Greek gods and goddesses once lived peacefully among humans on Earth. Over time, however, humans began to fight and behave badly. The gods became irritated. Most decided to leave and return to their heavenly home. Only Astraea stayed behind.

Astraea carried a set of scales with her. She used them to judge the good and evil she saw around her. As time went on, the fighting became worse. Eventually, Astraea decided to leave as well. Her father, Zeus, the king of the gods, placed her famous scales in the sky. Known as the Libra constellation, they remind everyone of the importance of balance and justice.

Even though Astraea left the wickedness of humanity behind, legend says that she will come back to Earth one day to return it to its peaceful state.

Libra and Cardinal Signs

In astrology, some zodiac signs share certain **qualities**. These qualities show how a person acts in the world. The qualities are separated into three groups. Cardinal signs are known for taking on leadership roles. Fixed signs make good business partners. Mutable signs are flexible. They can adapt to different situations.

Libra is a cardinal sign. People in this group are good at taking **initiative**. They are known for coming up with original ideas. Cardinal signs are confident. They know how to inspire others.

If cardinal signs see work that needs to be done, they are likely to jump in and do it. They will not wait to be told.

Zodiac Signs
by Quality

Cardinal Signs
Take on leadership roles.

Aries | Cancer | Libra | Capricorn

Fixed Signs
Make good business partners.

Taurus | Leo | Scorpio | Aquarius

Mutable Signs
Can adapt to different situations.

Gemini | Virgo | Sagittarius | Pisces

Know Your Libras

Libras continue to make an impact on the world. They can be found doing good work in various fields. Did you know these people are Libras?

Serena Williams

Born: September 26, 1981

Serena began playing tennis at the age of three, along with her sister Venus. She won her first **Grand Slam** tournament when she was just 18 years old. Since then, she has won another 22 Grand Slams in **singles** tennis. This is more than any other person. Serena also has four Olympic gold medals.

Serena won gold medals at the 2000, 2008, and 2012 Olympic Games.

Jenna Ortega

Born: September 27, 2002

This California-born actress landed her first **professional** role when she was only 9 years old. Jenna has been in demand ever since, acting in both film and television. In 2016, she was cast in her first starring role, as Harley Diaz in the **sitcom** *Stuck in the Middle*. This has led to parts in movies such as *The Babysitter 2* and *Saving Flora*.

Bruno Mars

Born: October 8, 1985

Bruno was born into a show-business family and spent his early years in Hawaii performing with them in local shows. His debut album was released in 2010 and quickly rose to the top of the charts. He has since performed to sold-out audiences around the world.

Kevin Durant

Born: September 29, 1988

Kevin's basketball prowess first became apparent in high school. After only one year of college basketball, he was **drafted** into the National Basketball Association (NBA). He joined the Golden State Warriors in 2016 and led the team to two NBA championships in a row. Kevin now plays with the Brooklyn Nets.

Zac Efron

Born: October 18, 1987

Zac rose to fame when he starred in the 2006 Disney movie *High School Musical*. He has gone on to star in a variety of movies ranging from comedies to serious dramas. His most recent project is the reality TV show *Killing Zac Efron*, which has him taking on several death-defying challenges.

The Libra QUIZ

1 How is a person's zodiac sign determined?

2 How many stars are in the main Libra constellation?

3 Who was Astraea?

4 Is Libra a cardinal, fixed, or mutable sign?

5 To which element group do Libras belong?

6 Which planet rules over Libra?

7 Which Libra athlete won four Olympic gold medals in tennis?

8 What three signs are considered love matches for a Libra?

ANSWERS: 1. By his or her date of birth 2. Six 3. A Greek goddess of justice and purity 4. Cardinal 5. Air 6. Venus 7. Serena Williams 8. Aquarius, Gemini, and Libra

Key Words

classical elements: materials from which all other materials were once believed to be made

compatible: able to exist together in harmony

constellations: groups of stars that form patterns in the sky

drafted: selected to play for a specific team

Grand Slam: the accomplishment of winning the four major tennis championships in one year

initiative: the ability to take action independently

intellectuals: people who have great mental capacity

orbit: a regular, repeating path that one object in space takes around another

professional: paid to do a job that people usually do as a hobby

qualities: traits that make a person or thing what it is

singles: a tennis game in which two players compete against each other

sitcom: short for situation comedy, a TV show in which the same characters are involved in amusing situations

Index

Get the best of both worlds.

AV2 bridges the gap between print and digital.

The expandable resources toolbar enables quick access to content including **videos**, **audio**, **activities**, **weblinks**, **slideshows**, **quizzes**, and **key words**.

Animated videos make static images come alive.

Resource icons on each page help readers to further **explore key concepts**.

Published by AV2
14 Penn Plaza 9th Floor
New York, NY 10122
Website: www.av2books.com

Library of Congress Control Number: 2020938561

ISBN 978-1-7911-2640-7 (hardcover)
ISBN 978-1-7911-2641-4 (softcover)
ISBN 978-1-7911-2642-1 (multi-user eBook)
ISBN 978-1-7911-2643-8 (single-user eBook)

Printed in Guangzhou, China
1 2 3 4 5 6 7 8 9 0 24 23 22 21 20

062020
101119

Editor: Heather Kissock
Designer: Terry Paulhus

AV2 acknowledges Getty Images, iStock, Shutterstock, Alamy, and Newscom as its primary image suppliers for this title.